Everyday 3-D Shapes

Prisms

by Laura Hamilton Waxman

illustrated by Kathryn Mitter

Content Consultant: Paula J. Maida, PhD,
Department of Mathematics, Western Connecticut State University

magic
wagon

visit us at
www.abdopublishing.com

 THIS BOOK CONTAINS AT LEAST 10% RECYCLED MATERIALS.

Text by Laura Hamilton Waxman
Illustrations by Kathryn Mitter
Edited by Rebecca Felix
Series design by Craig Hinton

Library of Congress Cataloging-in-Publication Data
Waxman, Laura Hamilton.
Prisms / by Laura Hamilton Waxman ; illustrated by Kathryn Mitter.
pages cm -- (Everyday 3-D Shapes)
Content Consultant: Dr. Paula Maida.
ISBN 978-1-61641-875-5
1. Prisms--Juvenile literature. 2. Shapes--Juvenile literature. 3. Geometry, Solid--Juvenile literature. I. Mitter, Kathy, illustrator. II. Title.
QA491.W378 2012
516'.156--dc23
2012007117

Prism ends match at top and base.

Each rectangle side is called a face.

Prism faces can't be round.

4

Curves and circles can't be found.

5

Look around for this shape's look.

Search for prisms in this book.

Breakfast starts the day out right.

Ben butters toast and takes a bite!

9

A row of prisms long and bright.

Jill sharpens one to draw and write.

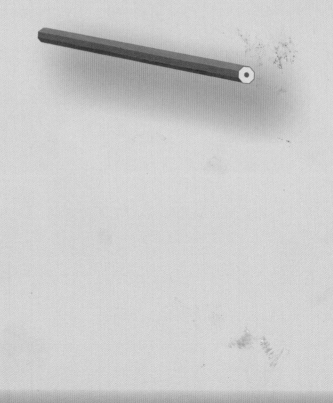

11

Prism beams both short and tall.

Ben is careful not to fall.

14

This prism is loud. *Bam! Bam! Boom!*

Which prisms make music in this room?

This prism box holds crackers to eat.

Add prisms of cheese for a tasty treat!

17

18

These prisms have sides that Jill sees through.

Candies inside are prisms, too!

Colorful prisms shaped the same.

Will Ben's green one win the game?

Prisms aren't just in this book.

22

They're all around you. Take a look!

I Spy a Prism Game

Look around. Find a prism. Then say, "I spy a prism that is . . ." and name its color. Everyone has to guess what prism you see. Then it is someone else's turn to spy a prism. You can guess what it is.

Count the Prisms Game

Choose a room in your home.
Count how many prisms you can find.

Glossary

base: the bottom of something.

prism: a shape that has flat faces and two ends of the same shape and size.

round: something that is circular in shape and has an equal distance from the center to any part of the edge.

shape: the form or look something has.